WEIRD SCIENCE

By Virginia Loh-Hagan

Disclaimer: This series focuses on the strangest of the strange. Have fun reading about strange people and things! But please do not try any of the antics in this book. Be safe and smart!

Published in the United States of America by Cherry Lake Publishing
Ann Arbor, Michigan
www.cherrylakepublishing.com

Reading Adviser: Marla Conn MS, Ed., Literacy specialist, Read-Ability, Inc.

Photo Credits: © Viki2win/Shutterstock.com, cover; Romanchuck Dimitry/Shutterstock.com, cover; anat chant/Shutterstock.com, cover; Valery Evlakhov/Shutterstock.com, cover; © Gucio_55/Shutterstock.com, 1, 26; © AndreasReh/iStock.com, 5; © Markus Gann/Shutterstock.com, 6; © NASA, 7; ©Ilya Sviridenko/Shutterstock.com, 8; ©Jackan/Shutterstock.com, 9; ©Liukov/iStock.com, 10; Gas Masks. , None. [Between 1909 and 1920] Photograph. Retrieved from the Library of Congress, https://www.loc.gov/item/npc2008000840/. (Accessed March 09, 2018.), 11; © World History Archive / Alamy Stock Photo, 12; © Eight Photo / Shutterstock.com, 14; © fmajor/iStock.com, 15; © JetKat/Shutterstock.com, 16; © RichVintage/iStock.com, 17; © USO/iStock.com, 18; © 20 David Tadevosian/Shutterstock.com, 20; ©kali9/iStock.com, 21; ©Bouillante/iStock.com, 22; © Juanmonino/iStock.com, 23; © Mario5B/Shutterstock.com, 24; ©George Marks/iStock.com, 25; ©CreativeNature_nl/iStock.com, 27; ©Everett Historical/Shutterstock.com, 28; ©l i g h t p o e t/Shutterstock.com, 30; ©David South / Alamy Stock Photo, 31

Graphic Element Credits: ©saki80/Shutterstock.com, back cover, front cover, multiple interior pages; ©queezz/Shutterstock.com, back cover, front cover, multiple interior pages; ©Ursa Major/Shutterstock.com, front cover, multiple interior pages; ©Zilu8/Shutterstock.com, multiple interior pages

45th Parallel Press is an imprint of Cherry Lake Publishing.

Library of Congress Cataloging-in-Publication Data has been filed and is available at catalog.loc.gov

Printed in the United States of America
Corporate Graphics

About the Author

Dr. Virginia Loh-Hagan is an author, university professor, former classroom teacher, and curriculum designer. Most of her science projects have gone wrong! She lives in San Diego with her very tall husband and very naughty dogs. To learn more about her, visit www.virginialoh.com.

Table of Contents

Introduction

Science is the study of all kinds of things. **Scientists** are people who study science. They study the world. They study nature. They study animals. They study people. They study forces. They study energy.

Scientists **observe**. Observe means to see. Scientists **experiment**. Experiment means to test things out. Scientists explore ideas. They design projects. They make many mistakes. They learn from their mistakes. They keep working. They want to get it right.

But there are science mistakes. And then, there are really strange science mistakes. These science mistakes are super strange. They're so strange that they're hard to believe. They sound like fiction. But these stories are all true!

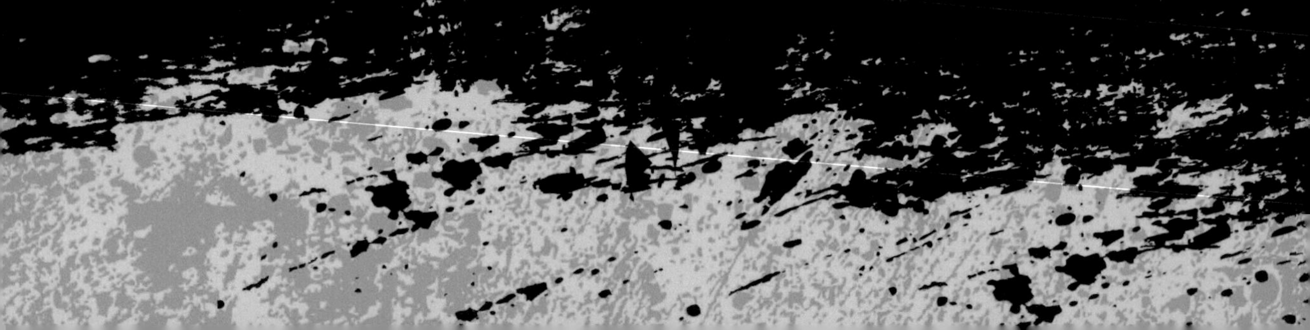

Some scientists work in labs. Some work in the field.

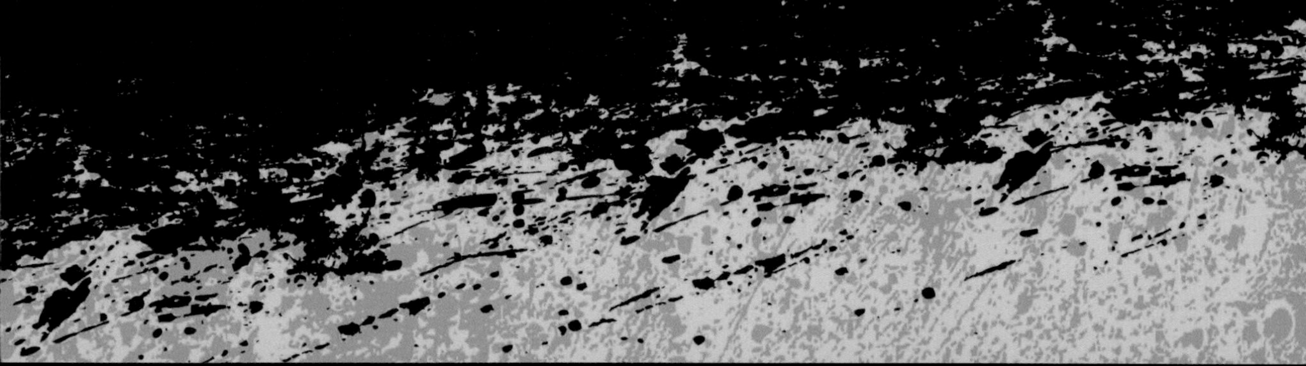

chapter one

NASA Probe

NASA manages space programs for the United States. It made a **probe**. Probes are like small rocket ships. NASA's probe was called *Genesis*. Its job was to go beyond Earth's moon. It was to bring back space material. It was launched in 2001. It was in space for 3 years. It collected bits from the sun's wind.

NASA scientists made a mistake. They put some parts in backward. The probe didn't know it was slowing down. So, it didn't launch a **parachute**. Parachutes look like large umbrellas. They help slow things down.

The plans were drawn backward.

The probe crashed in 2004. It crashed in Utah. This crash messed up the **samples**. Samples are bits. They were to be studied.

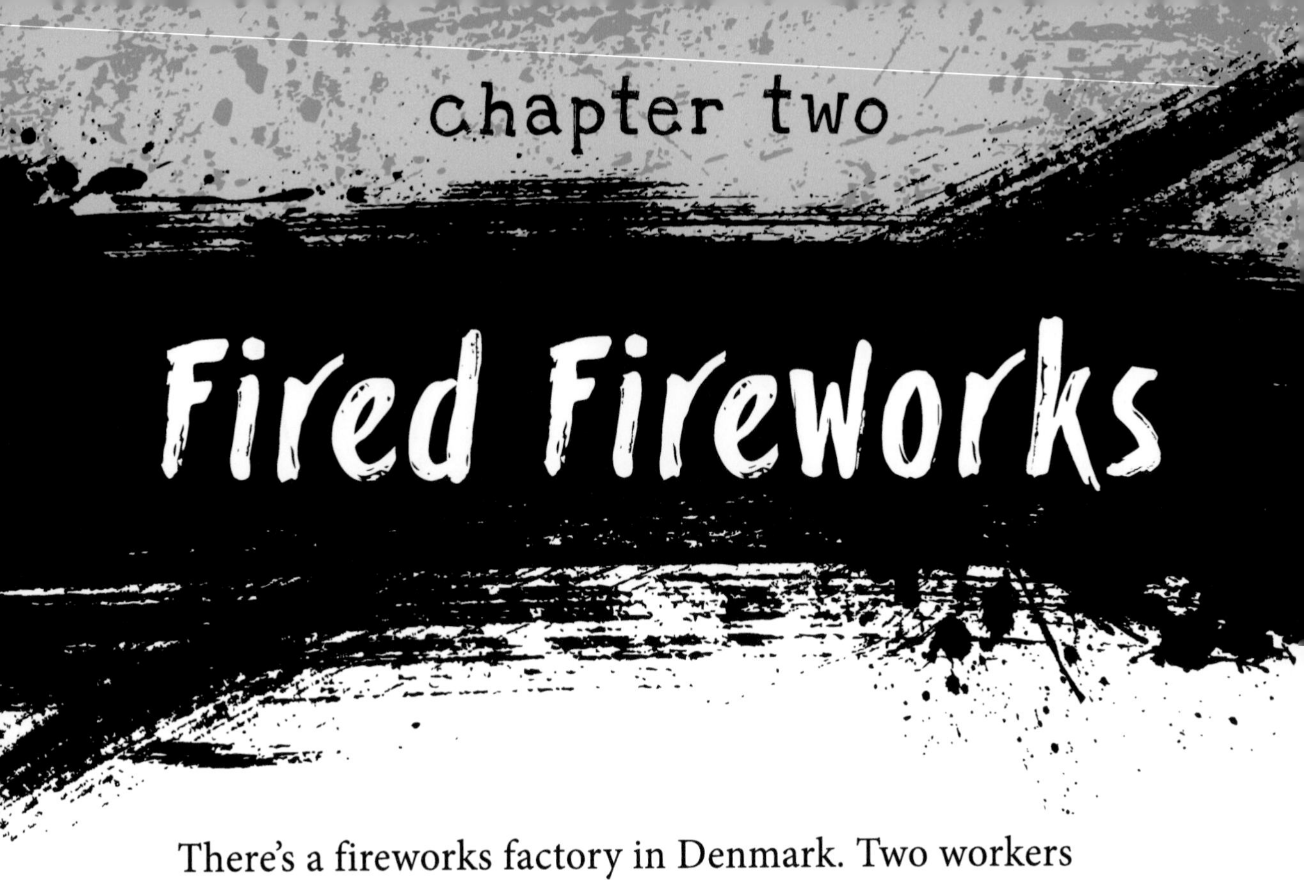

chapter two

Fired Fireworks

There's a fireworks factory in Denmark. Two workers dropped a box. There were fireworks in the box. The drop caused **friction**. Friction is a force. It's caused by rubbing. Friction set off the fireworks. This started a fire. The fire set off other fireworks. Every firework exploded. The factory had almost 300 tons of fireworks.

Over 2,000 buildings were destroyed. About 30 people were hurt. Many people had smoke in their lungs. One person died. Over 2,000 residents left the area. This saved their lives.

The Chinese invented fireworks.

This happened in 2004. An official said, “This looks worse than the many war zones I have seen.”

chapter three

Mustard Gas

Mustard gas is deadly. It burns skins. It burns eyes. It burns lungs. It causes sicknesses. It can be breathed in. It can be eaten. It can enter the body through the skin or eyes. It causes lifelong problems. It's used in war. It's used as a weapon.

The United States fought in World War II. The U.S. military was afraid of enemies using mustard gas. They wanted better protection. The U.S. Navy did experiments. They tested out gas masks. They tested out safety suits. First, they used animals. But that didn't work. So, they used humans. They used their own soldiers as **subjects**. Subjects are targets of tests.

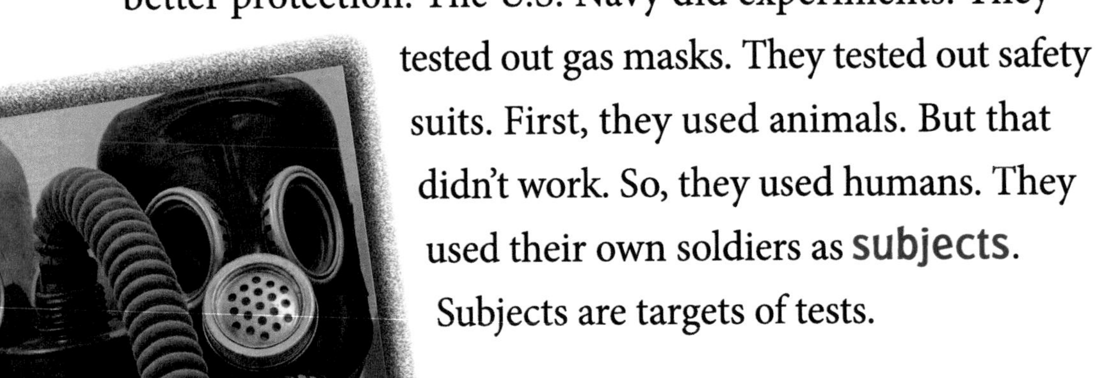

There is no known cure for mustard gas poisoning to date.

Navy sailors were asked to join a top secret experiment. They were told this would help shorten the war. The sailors wanted to help. They said yes. Later, they found out they were exposed to mustard gas. This happened in 1942.

Three types of experiments were done. First, mustard gas was put on skin. Second, subjects were exposed to mustard gas outside. Third, subjects were locked in rooms. Mustard gas was piped in. It looked like snow. One subject said, “It felt like fire.” Some soldiers didn’t want to do the tests. They were sent to jail. They were jailed for 40 years. These scientists hurt people. They broke laws. They weren’t honest. They weren’t safe.

The U.S. Army wouldn’t use their own men.

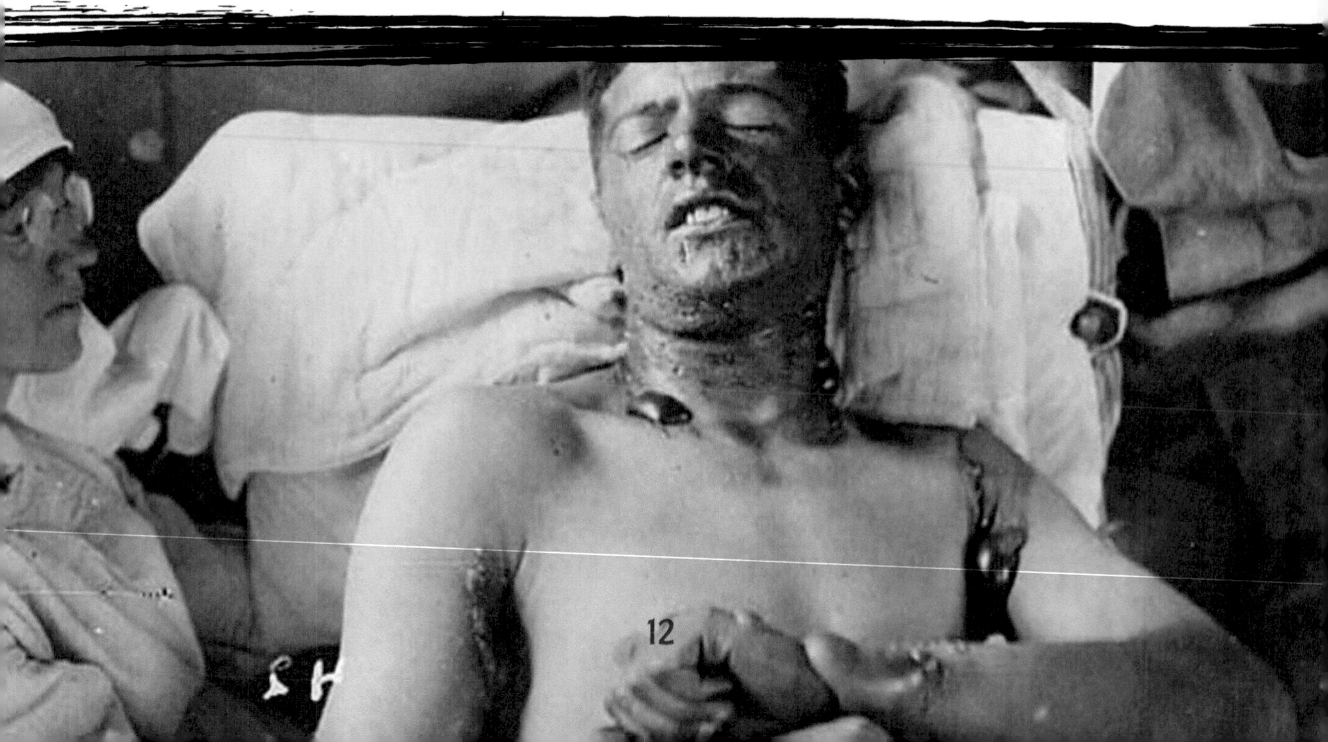

Explained by Science

Mistakes are made in science. Sometimes, small mistakes can mess up a science project. There are different types of mistakes. First, people make mistakes. This is called human error. An example is misreading data. Another example is not doing correct math. Another example is spilling or breaking things. Second, there are wrong calibrations. Calibration is a process. Scientists must make sure their tools are accurate. They make sure tools give the right data. Third, confirmation bias is an issue. This is when scientists do experiments to confirm what they already know. This means scientists aren't learning. They're not open to new ideas. They miss facts. They just want to be right.

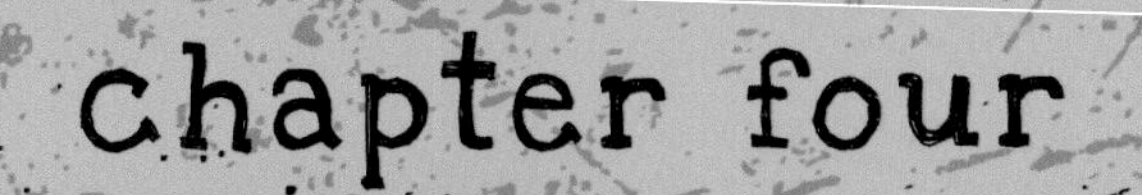

chapter four

Chernobyl Explosion

Pripyat is a city. It's in northern Ukraine. It used to have 50,000 people. But something bad happened. The Chernobyl nuclear power plant exploded. Workers messed up. They were testing how the plant would work if it lost power. They ran the plant at low power. They didn't follow safety rules. This made the power unstable. The power surged. Heat increased. Gas tubes blew up. Gas mixed with water. Water boiled. Steam exploded. Fire burned for 9 days.

This happened in 1986. **Radiation** was released into the air. This is bad energy. It's poisonous. Many people died. They were burned. They got sick.

Pripyat will be unsafe for at least 24,000 years.

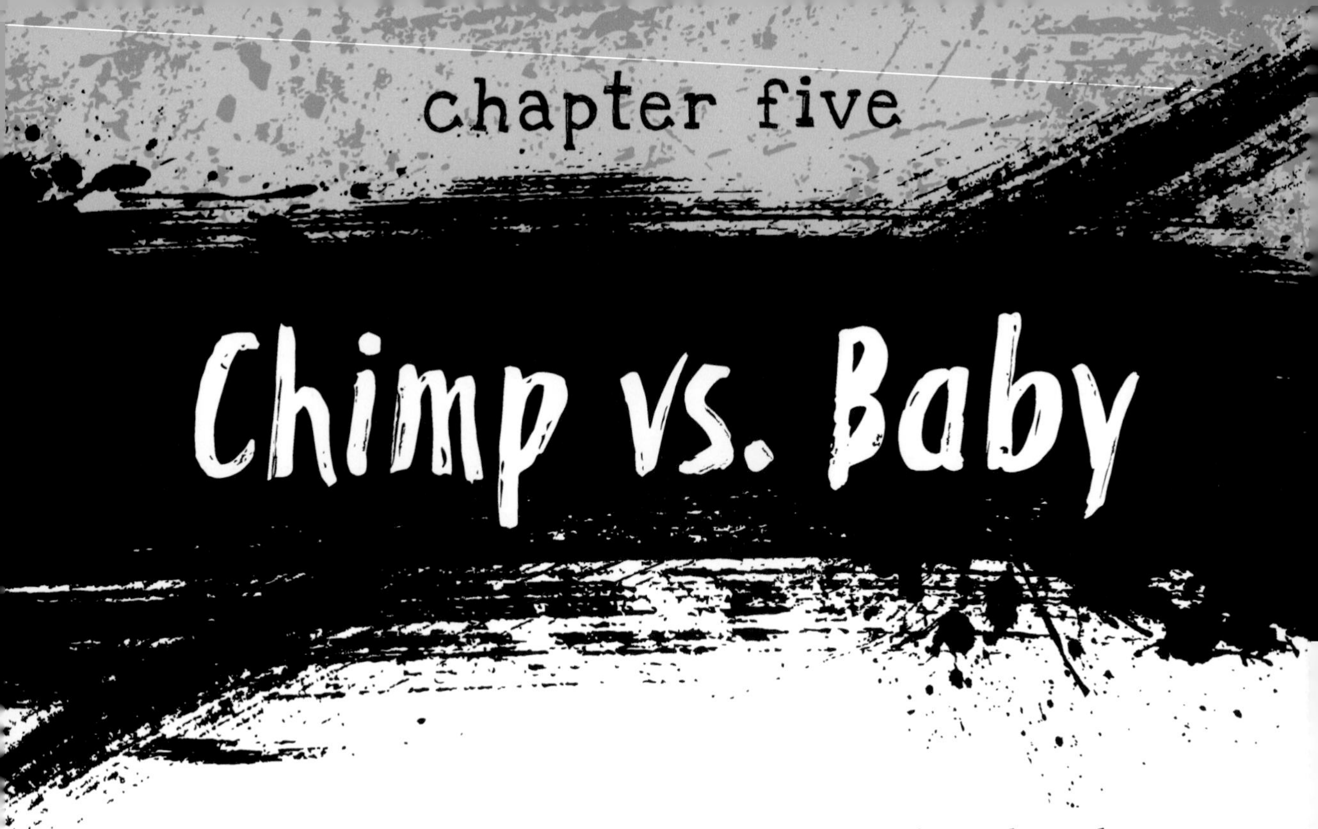

chapter five

Chimp vs. Baby

Luella and Winthrop Kellogg were scientists. They adopted Gua. Gua was a baby **chimpanzee**. Chimpanzees are also called chimps. They're apes. Gua was born in 1930.

The Kelloggs treated Gua like a human baby. They also had a son. The son's name was Donald. Gua and Donald were treated like twins. They were treated the same way. Gua was 7 months old. Donald was 10 months old.

The Kelloggs studied how environment influenced growth. They wanted to see if Gua could be more human. They wanted

Apes are the animals closest to humans.

Gua to speak. They wanted Gua to pick up human ways. They wrote a lot of notes. They recorded everything. They did a lot of tests.

They worked 12 hours a day. They worked 7 days a week. The experiment went well at first. Gua walked on two legs. She learned to use a spoon. She learned to use a cup. At age 1, she was doing more than Donald. Chimps mature faster than humans. They learn things more quickly. This made Gua look smarter.

This experiment lasted 9 months. The Kelloggs had to stop. Donald started acting like a chimp. He didn't learn a lot of words. He made chimp noises.

Gua was separated from Donald. She got sick. She died in 1933.

Gua was given to a research center in Florida.

Spotlight Biography

Stubbins Ffirth was a mad scientist. He was born in 1784. He was an American doctor. He studied yellow fever. He said it wasn't contagious. Contagious means spreading to others. He said people got yellow fever from stress and the summer heat. He tested these ideas. He cut his arms. He took vomit from people with yellow fever. Vomit is throw up. Yellow fever victims' vomit is black. Ffirth put the vomit in his cuts. He also rubbed victims' blood, spit, and pee on his body. He never got sick. He thought this was proof for both ideas. But Ffirth was wrong about one idea. His yellow fever patients didn't get sick from stress and the summer heat. Carlos Finlay was a Cuban scientist. He found that only mosquitoes caused yellow fever. Ffirth had tested himself for no reason.

chapter six

School Fire

McAllen is a city. It's in Texas. Students were learning at school. They were in a science lab. They did an experiment. There was a fire. Rafael Balderas is the fire chief. He said a "science experiment gone wrong" may have caused the fire.

Twenty students were taken to the hospital. Their lungs were checked for smoke. No students were harmed. One teacher was hurt. The teacher had small burns. The burns were on the stomach. Tom Torkelson is the head of the school. He said, "The students are not at fault here. This is our responsibility." He offered to pay all doctor bills.

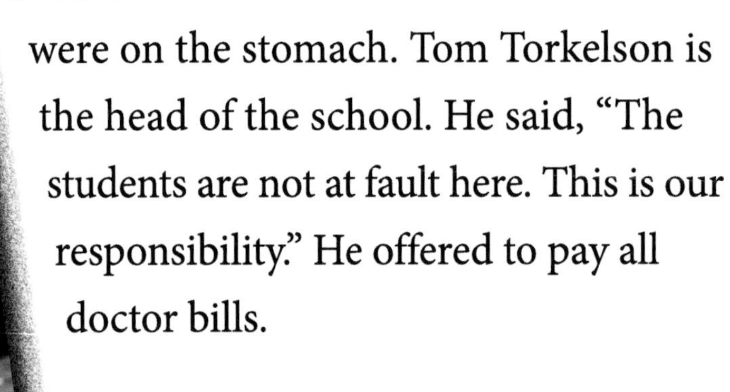

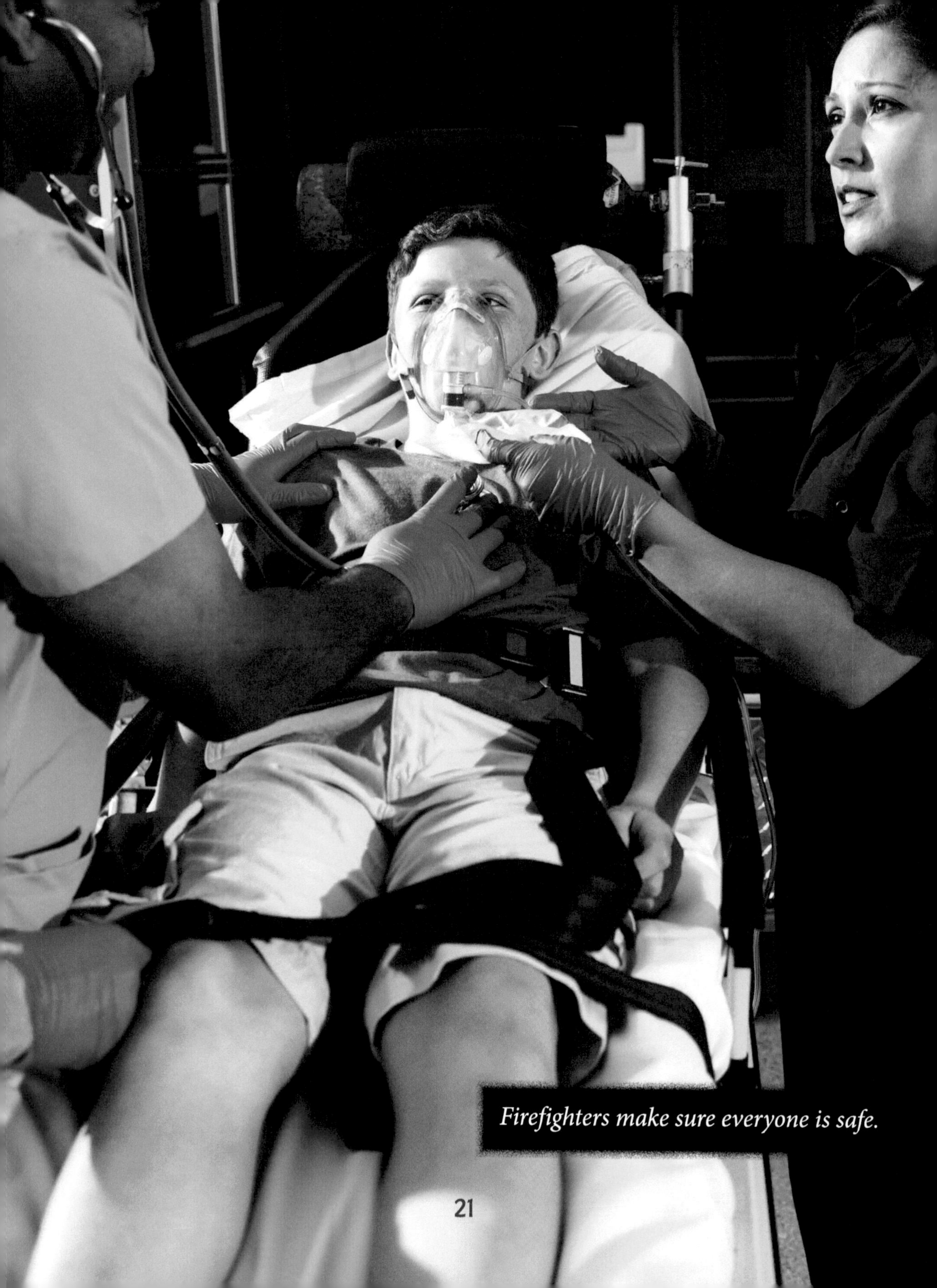

Firefighters make sure everyone is safe.

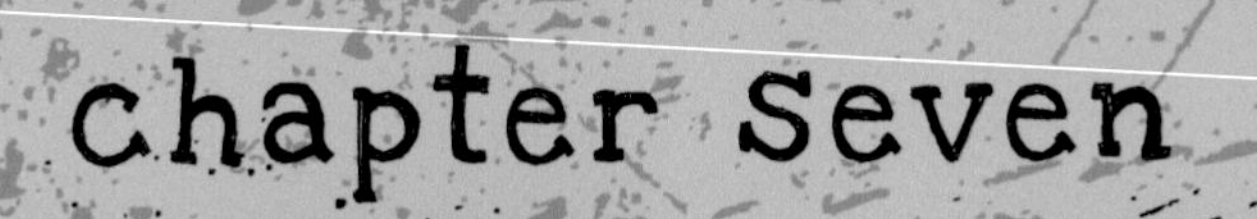

Chapter Seven

Elephants on Drugs

Louis West and Chester Pierce were scientists. They drugged an elephant. The elephant weighed 3½ tons. He was 14 years old. He lived in a zoo in Oklahoma City. He was given LSD. LSD is a drug. It causes **hallucinations**. Hallucinations are when people see things that aren't there. The elephant was given enough LSD for 3,000 people.

The elephant got scared. He panicked. He stamped around the pen. Then, he fell over. He died. This happened very quickly. This happened in 1962.

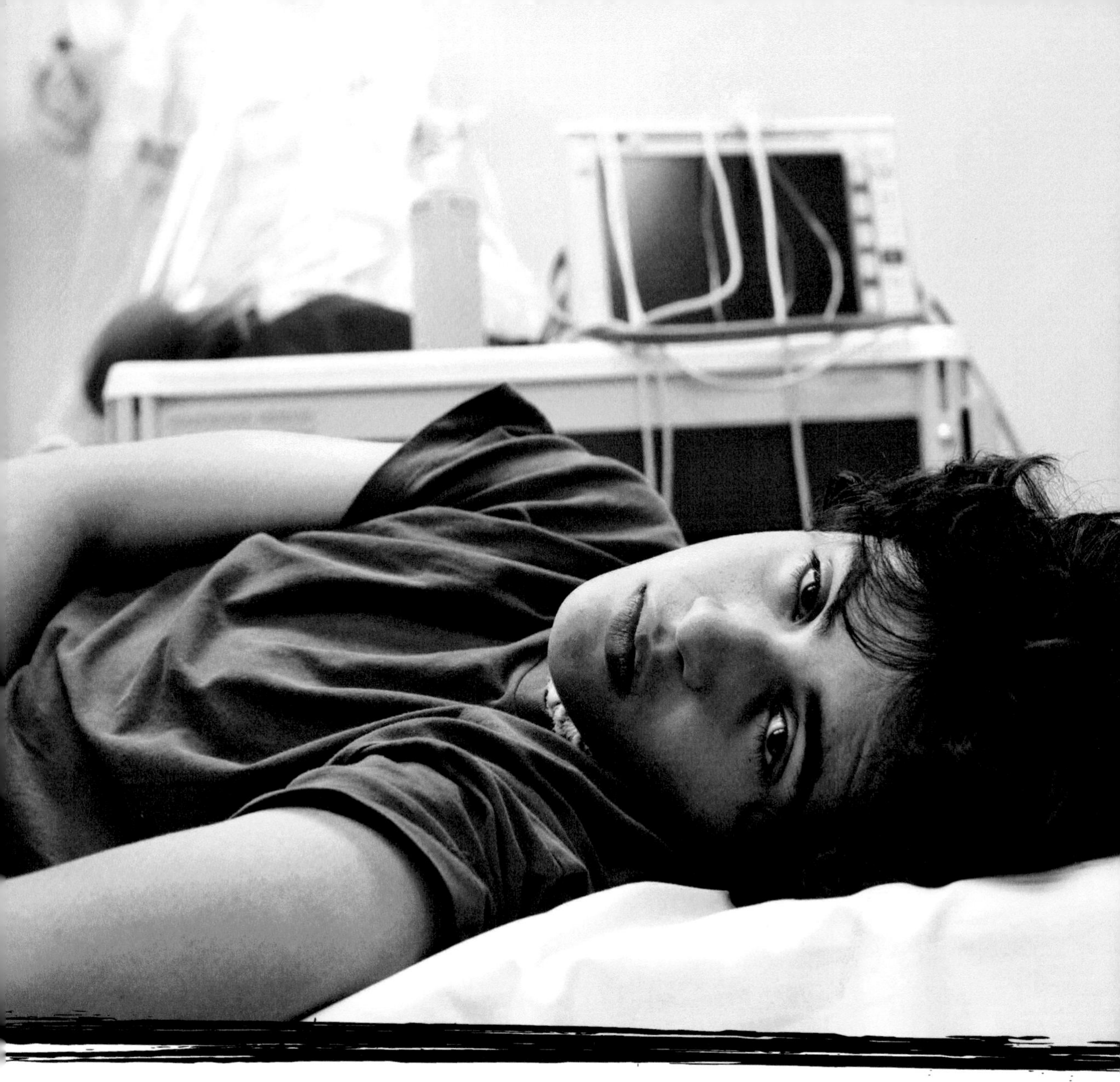

Taking drugs is dangerous.

Many people were mad at the scientists. West and Pierce fought back. They said it was supposed to be safe.

chapter eight

Monster Study

Wendell Johnson **stuttered**. Stuttering is the repeating of sounds. It's a speech problem. Johnson studied stuttering. He did many experiments. He used electric shock. He tested brain signals. He thought stuttering was learned.

He and Mary Tudor studied the effects of **feedback** on speech. Feedback is a response to something someone is doing. They studied 22 **orphans**. Orphans are children without parents. Johnson and Tudor gave half of the children positive feedback. They gave the other half negative feedback. They messed up the lives of children given negative

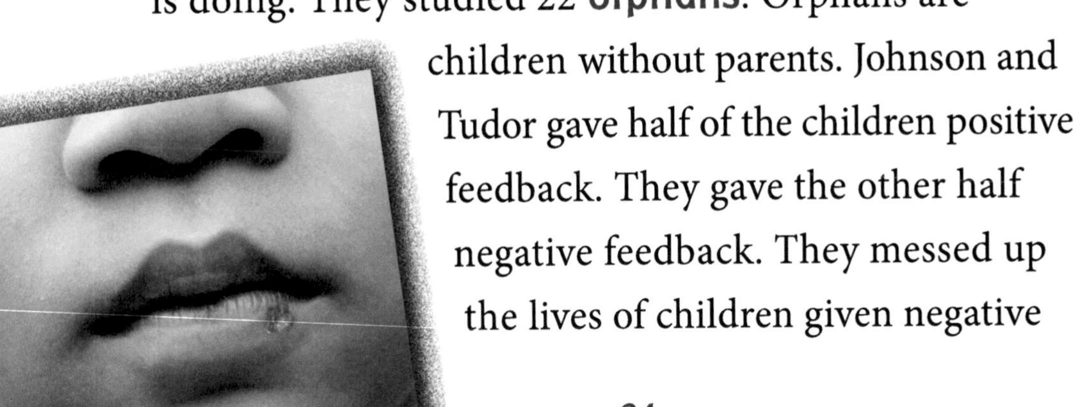

The study took place in Iowa in 1939.

feedback. The children developed speech problems. Other scientists were mad at Johnson and Tudor. They called it a "monster study."

chapter nine

Bat Bombers

Lytle Adams was a dentist. He came up with an idea. He talked to the U.S. president. His idea was for bat bombers. This was for World War II.

Bats could be flown in planes. They could be dropped from 5,000 feet (1,524 meters). They would fall over Japanese buildings. They would be carrying little bombs. The bombs could start fires. Japanese buildings were made of paper and wood. These would easily catch fire.

Science supported this idea. First, bats travel in groups. Second, bats carry twice their size. Third, bats **hibernate**.

The bat bombers experiment was called Project X-Ray.

Hibernate means to sleep during winter. They can be easily shipped. Scientists put bats in ice cube trays. Bats thought it was winter. Fourth, bats fly in darkness. They stay secret.

Louis Fieser was a scientist. He created the bat bomb and **carrier**. Carriers hold things. Each carrier held 40 bats. It opened and released bats.

Scientists did tests. One test was at an air base. Armed bats were accidentally let go. This started a fire. Another test took place. Bats fell to the ground. They dropped like stones. The United States stopped working on bat bombers. They focused on the **atomic** bomb instead. Atomic means powerful energy.

Regular bombs could start 400 fires. Bat bombers could start 5,000 fires.

Try This!

- Do a science project. Follow the scientific method. First, ask a question. Second, make a prediction. Third, collect data. Fourth, test things out. Fifth, make conclusions.
- Watch videos of science experiments. Try some yourself. Be safe. Wear protective gear. Don't handle dangerous things.
- Read about a science topic. Ask questions. Think about what more you want to know.
- Talk to a scientist. Learn more about his or her research.
- Talk to a science teacher. Ask what he or she likes about science.
- Take a walk outside. Ask lots of questions. Write them down. Explore one of the questions. Remember, science is all around you.

chapter ten

Killer Bees

Killer bees were made by man. This happened in the 1950s. Warwick Kerr is a scientist. He's from Brazil. He studied bees. He crossed two types of bees. European honey bees are friendly. African honey bees are meaner. They like to fight. They make more babies. They build hives faster. Kerr thought African honey bees would be better for South American weather. But he wanted nicer bees.

He combined the two types of bees. He wanted more honey. He wanted to breed the meanness out of the bees. But some African bees escaped. They bred with local bees. They were meaner. These

Kerr's assistant is blamed for letting the bees escape.

killer bees flew north. In 1990, killer bees were found in Texas. They spread to California. They've killed over 1,000 people. They've killed animals.

Consider This!

Take a Position! Scientists learn by trial and error. They learn by doing science. They learn by making mistakes. Are mistakes good or bad? Argue your point with reasons and evidence.

Say What? Do research. Find another example of science gone wrong. Describe what happened. Explain the science behind the project.

Think About It! Scientists need to have high standards. They must base ideas on data. They can't get caught up in their own thoughts. They must give up on ideas that aren't supported by data. Think about a time that you used data to support your ideas. Think about a time that you did not use data to support your ideas.

Learn More!

- Editors of YES Mag. *Hoaxed! Fakes and Mistakes in the World of Science.* Tonawanda, NY: Kids Can Press, 2009.
- Jones, Charlotte Foltz, and John O'Brien (illust.). *Mistakes That Worked: 40 Familiar Inventions and How They Came to Be.* New York: Delacorte Books for Young Readers, 1994.
- Zuchora-Walske, Christine. *That Bull Is Seeing Red! Science's Biggest Mistakes About Animals and Plants.* Minneapolis: Lerner Publications, 2014.

Glossary

atomic (uh-TAH-mik) powerful energy created by splitting atoms

carrier (KAR-ee-ur) something that holds other things

chimpanzee (chim-pan-ZEE) a type of ape

experiment (ik-SPER-uh-ment) to test out

feedback (FEED-bak) written or spoken reactions to something you are doing

friction (FRIK-shuhn) force that creates heat or energy by rubbing

hallucinations (huh-loo-suh-NAY-shuhnz) the seeing of things that aren't there

hibernate (HYE-bur-nate) to sleep during winter

observe (uhb-ZURV) to see, to study by seeing

orphans (OR-fuhnz) children who do not have living parents

parachute (PAH-ruh-shoot) a large piece of thin fabric attached to ropes that spreads out in the air to slow down something as it falls to the ground

probe (PROHB) small rocket ship sent to discover or find something

radiation (ray-dee-AY-shuhn) energy that is released into the air

samples (SAM-puhlz) bits of something used for study

scientists (SYE-uhn-tists) people who study an area of science

stuttered (STUHT-urd) to repeat sounds, a speech problem

subjects (SUHB-jikts) targets of experiments, participants of a study

Index